YELLOW WOMAN SPEAKS

Selected Poems
Expanded Edition

AF271785

RADICAL WOMEN Publications
Seattle, WA

MERLE WOO

Radical Women National Office: New Freeway Hall
5018 Rainier Ave. S., Seattle, WA, USA
(206)722-6057• Fax (206)7237691
RadicalWomenUS@gmail.com • www.radicalwomen.org

© 2003 Radical Women Publications
5018 Rainier Avenue South, Seattle, WA 98118, USA
(206)722-6057 • Fax (206)723-7691
rwseattle@mindspring.com

Expanded edition 2003
First edition published 1986
by Radical Women Publications

ISBN 0-9725403-6-9

Editor: Helen Gilbert
Design: Anya Willow

Poems © Merle Woo
Photos of Merle Woo: Cover foreground photo by
Mary Ann Curtis, 1997. Cover background photo by
Cathy Cade, 1981. Photo on page 57 by Jean Weisinger
from *Imagery: Women Writers, 1996.*

Thanks to the editors of the following publications,
in which many of these poems originally appeared:
*Plexus, The Haight-Ashbury Literary Journal, The Asian
American Journey, Breaking Silence: An Anthology of
Contemporary Asian American Poets, Forkroads, The
Forbidden Stitch, The Arc of Love, My Lover is a Woman,*
and *Sing, Whisper, Shout and Pray!*

Contents

Korea

My grandmother named her Korea. The oldest girl in the family.
The exact year of her birth is still in question. Maybe 1896.
You see, it was an obsession with her to keep her age from
     everyone;
she even changed her birth certificate.

Since she was the only one of her eight children who was
     born in their home country, grandmother had named her
     Korea.

Korea Chang.

Although she thought my mother, her little sister Helen,
     ugly, she loved her in a sometimes cruel way, and
they were always close all their lives,
all over the world.

My mother Helen —
Wanted a more glorious, beautiful and romantic life.
Didn't want to be just a plain old "Helen."
So my mother changed her name to Helene.

But, Korea Chang:

She grew up in Shanghai. My mother was there too.
The park outside the International Zone had a sign that said:
"No Dogs. No Chinamen."

     Korea Chang changed her name to Cora Chandler to live
     better in the world.

And she was so beautiful:

     Had the strong high cheekbones of Korea —
     and eyes — big, round and full,

but with a hint of Korea.
She dyed her hair to a flaming red,
until the roots turned grey, and then dyed it silver.
Wore sea-green, silver-flecked mascara —
Cora Chandler with her false eyelashes,
White face makeup and rouge over the high cheekbones.

Came to the U.S. single and with a baby girl —
    Named Gloria — after Swanson
    (Later had Wally — after Beery)

Popular with men, with sailors —
    In her sunglasses worn all the time,
    shading the beautiful dark eyes.

How she took care of her face:

    Cold cream every night, told my mother —

    "Now, Helene—cream and lotion every night
    on the places age hits the most: the hands, neck, elbows.
    Cover the forehead! Keep the deadly wrinkles away."

    The wrinkles will keep the men away. Success away.

My mother followed in her footsteps, naming two of her
children in the same fashion —

    Ronald — after Colman
    Merle — after Oberon

But mother wouldn't, couldn't hide her heritage.
Married Chinese, had Korean-Chinese children.

You know, we couldn't visit my Auntie Cora in San Mateo
    while we were growing up.

She feared the neighbors finding out —
Might be suspicious if they saw a bunch of Asians

climbing out of an old Buick and going into her house.

I would sit under the table while Helene and Cora talked
at our flat in San Francisco.

Of men, work, family.
Reminiscing about their lives as young women:

How Helene with her retarded daughter, Christina,
stayed with Cora. And while Cora worked in a factory,
Helene kept the tiny apartment, taking care of their
two girl-children.

Two single mothers —
Korean women in Chicago during the '20s.

I loved their stories,
My aunt's biting humor and sharp tongue —
Made me laugh.

Stories about her kind of people at the horse races,
Reno: gamblers, prostitutes, lesbians.

Even as a teenager, I would still drift in to hear their talk.

Oh, she did become bitter over the years.
Sarcastic tones in all her phrases —
Words like "fat," "ugly," "pig," "poor" and "stupid" —
referring to her family.

Her succession of houses, a descension into poverty.
Dying of stomach cancer, fragile and broken,
in Nairobi, East Palo Alto.

How I admired this woman:

She loved me and treated me good,
always giving me talcum powder in pink satin boxes,
and pungent perfumes in exotic glass bottles,

racy negligees in sizes too big.
She taught me that life is harsh —
Taught me to fight with whatever tools I had.

She used her looks and the values she had no choice but to accept.

One tool I have is the message of her life —
And that tool is really a weapon.

China

For Nellie Wong

China.

What does that word mean to the Chinese American
     generations away?

Does it mean great expanses of land —
     warlords, feudal kingdoms, wild horses,
     women soldiers, concubines of emperors?

     Jagged mountains,
     melting snow forming into misty waterfalls,
     the tiny human small against Chinese nature —

     The silkscreens so familiar in the windows
     of art shops in our American Chinatowns?

     Jade dragons and goddesses,
     the red, gold and greens of embroidered peacocks,
     ivory horses and elephants,

     Or the richest of foods, the best in the world?

*My comrade is going to our ancestors' land
     and I don't know what that means.*

China.

How will it feel to be among thousands who are the
     same color as we?
And to walk on the soil of the people who gave us
     life, culture, manners,
     the perspective of poor peasants —
     now lost in the dimness of some vague, untouchable memory.

Will it be better or worse than the pictures we've seen,
    the history we've read,
    the stories we've heard from people who've gone back.

Does it mean Mao Zedong and the long, long march —
    the line a magnet —
    gathering the millions of peasants and workers
    leaving what little they had behind,
    pulled into a perilous journey to a precarious freedom?

Or the feminist Ding Ling,
    the courageous writer and worker being censored for
    decades —
    a victim of both the Kuomindong and the Chinese
    Communist Party?

Will my sister, an American visitor,
    feel the kinship with the majority of the people of the world?

A people who have endured wars and exploitation —
    the natural disasters of earthquakes, drought and famine?
A changing revolutionary country which is scarred
    by an opportunistic bureaucracy?

We the children of Asian immigrants.

Happy, contented people have no reason to leave their homeland.
So ours is the legacy of the starving poor,
    the persecuted and exploited peasant,
    and the contempt of women.

In China,
    Nellie will see:
    Chinese children,
    workers,
    doctors,
    farmers,
    officials,
    women.

Nellie will observe the women.
And they will observe Nellie the Chinese American.

What will they know of us?

Will they understand racism?
    The legacy of the despised Chinaman in America?
    The 101 laws against us —
    The depth and breadth of the racism and sexism
    against the American-born Asian working woman?

    Will they know what it means to be a wave of yellow
    in a sea of white?

    The lies, distortions, never being seen as we are?

What will be the bond?

It won't be language or culture —

    Maybe our eyes, our skins, our black hair —
    perhaps the commonality of being treated as women.

There is so much meaning in going *there*.
    Not *back*.
    But there, to a continent called China.

We, in our forties, second generation,
    growing up assimilated into white America,
    but getting the chance to mature into revolutionists.
    A rare opportunity to exercise human potential.

We, the proud Asian American women
Asian the adjective
American the identity —

Nellie Wong, going to China,
    goes for me too.

A Liŋwistək Song for My Comrades

You are my Tibetan Numerals,
My dear Squamish Vowels —

We are in complementary distribution
from the Atlantic to the Pacific.
Allophones of the same
Phoneme:

Freedom

Class Szechuan-Style

Szechuan Village for me and Paul
We order hot-braised fish Szechuan style
and sautéed fresh spinach —
A meal fit for champions.

Paul is my son. He's fourteen.
Sometimes by way of introduction,
I say, "I'm Paul's mother. I'm forty."

He runs over to the 7/11 to play one game of Scramble,
and I sit and listen.
I wonder why I listen to the people who are eating in
Chinese restaurants.
I overhear a white businessman and his wife entertaining a
businessman from Hong Kong.

The white man says, "I bet I know more about Chinese
languages than you do. I studied them!"
He ticks off a list of Cantonese dialects.
Gives a short lecture on Mandarin.
The Chinese businessman nods to their observations about
Peking duck, the majesty of Kow Loon.
He is so obsequious.
Laughing and totally accommodating.

I say something about the white couple to Paul,
who's just come back.
He listens.
Paul says, "And the Asian guy is so ignorant! So ignorant!
If he was native American, they wouldn't do that to him!"
I say, "Yeah, but he knows.
 I wonder how many times a week he has to go through
that routine."

A Young Filipino comes over and squats down beside me.

"Hey. I was in your EOP English class years ago at S.F. State.
How you doin? Remember me? I'm Vince."
He's squatting there easy,
elbows on thighs, hands hanging loosely clasped together.
Easy.

He's wearing jeans, an old weathered leather jacket,
navy-blue sweatshirt protruding around the collar;
he's got on round black wire-rimmed glasses.
His wife is smiling two tables from me.

"Yeah, well I quit school a couple semesters after I took your class."
"Not relevant?" I ask.
"Not relevant? No. I had to leave and go to work full-time.
Had to support the family. Couldn't get no more Financial Aid.
But it's been pretty good. I'm happy."

"Where you workin?" I ask.
"At SF Airport. United. Baggage."
He asks, 'You still at State?"
"No."
I tell Vince I've been at U.C. Berkeley now for over 3 years.
In Asian American Studies.
He says, "Really moved up then?"
Paul laughs.
"It's actually been really hard," I reply.
Courses are being eliminated.
Political content being watered down.
Tutors, lecturers, and staff who were openly critical of the
program have been fired.

Vince gets up and sits on a chair at the empty table beside us.
He says, "It's always been hard, hasn't it? Geez!"
He goes on, "I thought I had it hard, but man,
it must be harder for you!"
I don't know if I agree. It's all the same.

I hear a soft laugh. A Japanese American woman at the table
right next to Vince's is smiling at us.

14

She's got on a white silk blouse and is quite elegant.
The man with her is wearing a bone-colored wool suit.
He's got a mustache.
She says, "You won't believe this, but I was in your freshman
class at U.C. the first year you were there.
I was in 6A. Remember me? I'm June."
(I'm thinking, so you're graduating this year, and maybe
I'm leaving too.)
"Gonna graduate this year?" I ask.
"Yes. In Japanese. We're leaving for Japan in July."

Paul and I sit around yakking and digesting.
I ask my fortune cookie, "What's going to happen to me this
year?"
It says, "You will inherit much money and jewelry."
Paul says, "Well, that's irrelevant."
He puts the left-over fish in a gee-hop, meticulously picking
out the bones.
We talk about school. His and mine.
I say, "And we don't even have Free Speech!"
He says, "I thought you were into Women's liberation.
Don't let them push you around."
Then he adds, "Boy, all your fans were here."

On the way home, I'm thinking how proud I was
in front of Paul.
Here's part of my work right in front of him.
I touched their lives somehow.

Vince and I:
we saw each other for fifteen weeks, MWF from 2-3. One
spring semester.
San Francisco State. Educational Opportunity Program.

From Fall of 1969 —
Bertha - Black
Art - Black
Anita - Brown
Jeff - Yellow

Teresa - Red
and Me.
We were the core of teachers.

To Spring, 1978 —
I saw each of them go or get fired, one by one.
Until there was only me.
They kept me, because I am an Asian woman.
I was an accommodating, non-confrontive, academic
Asian woman.
Each time one left, there were the words:
"Should we do something?
Write a letter of enraged criticism of the racism here?"
But no. . .
We need recommendation letters and what would they
do to you
the ones who are left?
The one who is left?

When I left after 9 years, there was no one to say goodbye to.
9 years of invisibility.
Sue, the EOP counselor said,
"So, you're splitting on us, too!"
I left to find a better position.

June and I met MW from 8-10. Fall Quarter, 1978.
Asian American Studies Six Series.
A collective of 28 tutors and 4 lecturers.
We now have 8 tutors and me: a socialist feminist and
a lesbian.
This time as we saw them go,
as we saw democratic decision-making, student participation go,
We fought back together.

From meetings in the tutor room, 363 Dwinelle,
with its reds, oranges, and blues of community posters
— Yellow People's History —
memorabilia and pictures
of old tutor potlucks and softball games,

to open criticism, asking questions,
articles in newspapers,
teach-ins, boycotts,
red armbands and red balloons drifting over Sproul with the words:
"Save Asian American Studies."
Mass meetings, skits,
everyone speaking out: defending me, defending us,
defending our basic right for democracy and a real education.

"June's smart," says Paul.
"That's right. But, hell, they're all smart."
He says, "Yeah, but she is smart.
Do you know how many Japanese characters there are?
A thousand!
And now there's this new computerized typesetting machine
that squirts ink out
through tiny needles to make those letters!"

We drive Route 280 home.
And I think, this time it will be different.
Whether we go or stay,
our course will be directed by:
integrity, visibility, and revolutionary possibility.

The Subversive

For Nellie Wong

She rides a broom and curses God —
She gets burned at the stake if
    she isn't run through with it;
Her name is spoken in whispers because
    she has killed her children rather than
    let them starve —

She has no grace and swaggers;
picks her teeth with a dirty fingernail.
She's pushy and loud —
a voice like shirt buttons on a washboard.
How we hate her style —

We forget that she's helping us
    get what we want!
We forget because we're so busy
    being embarrassed and downright ashamed —
because she criticizes and yells,
    pointing a red stubby finger —

How gross! Send her back!
Let's just send her back right where she came from!

Poem for the Creative Writing Class, Spring 1982

The silence in the classroom
of people I've grown to respect —
seems like so much potential here:
men and women
brown black yellow jewish white
gay and straight.

Classrooms are ugly,
cages with beautiful birds in them.
scraped, peeling walls
empty bookcases
an empty blackboard —
no ideas here.

And one window.
One writer comes in
from sitting on the sill,
three stories up.
We all want to fly
and feel the sun on the backs of our wings —

Inhale the breath
pulling in the energy of
seventeen people around me
and exhale
putting out my ideas, ideas, ideas.
We all want to fly out that window.
A breeze comes in once in a while
we want to go out with it
to where the birds are.

To take flight
using the words
that give us wings.

What is language after all
but the touching and uplifting
one to the others:
scenes
poems
dreams
our own natural imagery:
coins
a train to El Salvador
sleeping, pregnant mothers
menacing garages/a fist pounding/voices yelling
a yogi
cops being the bowery boys
roller coasters
blood
a girl on a swing
roses
water, streams, rivers, oceans
rise. rise.

Who can keep us caged?

For Dick Woo (Woo Nay)

In my dream he sits in a wheelchair behind a veil. Old and withered in a white gown. I am small and want to crawl under the veil to touch him. He is playing a guitar. (I have never seen him play an instrument in my life.)

On Angel Island for a year and a half. Came when he was 13. A paper son. Went back home to China with his aging dying father. Came back when 20. Already with a wife there.

He once worked 2 jobs: an accountant and a butcher for Sang Wo & Company (at Grant and Washington).
Strong wrists and fingers loudly flipping the beads on the abacus. With the other tool — the butcher knife — he could chop garlic and vegetables a million pieces a minute and round ducks into delicious small rectangles.

Sang Wo was noisy and smelly. Sawdust on the red floor. Customers and workers yelling, laughing in abrasive Cantonese.

My father wrapping free food, usually cha siew or lop cheung in newspapers for friends, family. My friends said, "We can't just go in to say 'Hi' to your dad but he has to give us something."

At night a gambler. Could tell the mahjong tiles simply by rubbing his fingers on their faces. Met my mother waitressing at the Jackson Cafe where he would make his lottery connection by phone to Oakland.

Always dressed like a successful underworld gambler. Up to 6 months ago. Plaid jackets, silk shirts, red ties. From Jack Davis. Soft wool hats covering his always bald head. That's all he spent his money on. Didn't drink or smoke. "What a waste," we'd say. "He never goes anywhere except to the store. Doesn't know anything else."

When I was growing up on Powell Street near Clay, he had one big win. 1949 Christmas morning: a brand new Admiral TV. Dark rich mahogany cabinet.

Some Sundays he was off. We'd go to the S.F. zoo. (Huery Fly-shack-ah) Never talking. Just holding hands and eating peanuts. Or maybe 2 movies in one day. First to the Fox and then to the Golden Gate. Paul Muni/ "Scarface" his idol.

Never talked. Always distant. Me always saying I'm sorry. I'm Jook sing, you know.

Twenty years I'm out of my parents' home. Married. Divorced. 2 grown children.

I told my mother a few years ago that I'm a lesbian. She told him. He told her, "No Homosex in China." "But he's not surprised," she said, "because you're a Marxist."

November last year. Open heart surgery at 77 years. Very poor recovery. He scrawls on a pad of paper, "Where's my Bunny?" That being me because he can't say Merle. (Muh-lo)

For 6 months now, he has a trach tube in his throat. So he can't talk. He mouths Cantonese words we cannot understand; knocks on the cabinet with his knuckles. His lungs fill with mucus and blood after bouts of pneumonia and staph infections.

I sit by him. Try new words of Sam Yup I've learned from my Auntie Lula and comrade Nellie:
"Nay jow ho fan, lo." (You will get better soon.)
"Nay ho keurng jong." (You are very strong.)
"Gnaw jern ging nay." (I respect you.)
"Gnaw yow nee-gah sum." (Your heart is mine.)
He smiles and caresses my head.

I tell him I'm suing my boss for unfairly firing me. He leans over and solemnly shakes my hand. A Gentleman.

Not one of his old friends have come to see him in these 6 months. Superstition.

When he's not in isolation he sits in a wheelchair by the nurse's station, wanting to be in the middle of working people. But their words are not the words of Sang Wo: "Do you *understand*, Mr. Woo?"

For the first time in his life, he picks a flower. From the roof garden of the hospital. Displays the pink gardenia in a glass. He asks me to bring him a red flower. Red. For luck.
Lucky Goong Goong.

When they took him up to the 5th floor after being in the intensive unit, they tied his hands down in the bed. He panicked. Couldn't reach the nurse's bell. Stopped breathing.

Now it's been 2 months that he's been sitting up in a chair refusing to go to bed. Ghosts are in the walls, he says.

His feet swell up enormously. They put Jobst boots on. He gets ulcers on his legs. They put Saran Wrap on the necrotic area.

I have loved wiping his head in his fevers, and yes, rubbing his feet too — the skin tight like balloons filled with water — and cutting his nails and touching him.

I feel pain in seeing him suffer for so long,
away from the sounds of his community,
and joy that I can be close to him once again;
not having to talk,
feeling my father's need for his daughter.

Currents

During my lunch break, I walk in the pouring rain,
from where I work as a secretary
at Montgomery and Bush
to East/West Journal
at Grant Ave. and Washington.

Right across the street where my father was a butcher
at Sang Wo and Co.

I pass 25 banks on Montgomery in a four block walk.

I ride up to the third floor of the Empress of China building,
feeling a bit childish in my father's raincoat,
a cap and soaking corduroy pants,
to meet the friendly people of this Chinese American newspaper.

Virginia Mei has asked me for my Chinese name,
so East/West can translate the story of my case into Chinese.

But I don't know how to write my name —
I can only say it.

I have brought some calligraphy in black and red crayon,
hoping that this is it. Long ago, my son Paul had been taught
some Chinese by his 1st grade teacher, Sue Lim.

Virginia laughs at what I brought.
It says "Good Luck" or something like that.

Then she asks me to say my name.
I say, "Woo Suk Ying."

She says, "Hm. Let me try."
So she grabs a piece of paper and begins to write.

As she does so, I remember
the three dashes here, the little box there.
She has gotten my name!
I haven't seen it in years.

"How did you know? How did you know?"

The people there tease me and say,
"Oh, she's known you for a long, long time."

Virginia says, "It was easy, that's a common girl's name.
And you said it with the right accent. Just right."

How I beamed with pleasure.
Saying it right.
My name being a common girl's name.
Like the Asian American working woman that I am.

> ("Merle" is not a common girl's name because my mother
> didn't want me to be a common girl like she was.)

East/West is translating the story of my unfair termination
into Chinese. Benjamin Chan, a translator there, says they
want as much support for my reinstatement as possible.
Because I am a "minority and a lady."

Yes, indeed, and a lesbian, a unionist, and socialist feminist.
What are the characters for these words?

Virginia says, "Here, let me write your name down on another
piece of paper for you. Don't lose it now."

As I leave, Virginia says, "Thank you for coming in all this rain."

I say, "Thank you for giving me back my name."

I kept explaining to them:
I only went to Chinese school for one year and flunked.
I said, I don't know my name because my mother is Korean.

(Passing the buck to my mother.)

I said, Oh and I have every intention of learning Cantonese
very soon. Sure.

Always feeling I have to hide or make up excuses
when I say I don't understand:

    "Gnaw emhew gong tong-wah."

Students, staff and I got mad and protested when we lost
Cantonese and Tagalog in Asian American Studies, UCB.

    Got fired because we protested.
    Got mad when we lost the bilingual ballot.
    Faster and faster losing bilingual/bicultural
    maintenance in the schools.
    College counselors telling Third World students
    not to study bilingual ed.
    because there's no future in it,
    no projected funding.

Jesus. And I'm still apologizing.

I prefer to walk back to work along Grant Ave.

Twice as many art and dry goods stores on Grant
as banks on Montgomery.

I can imagine a wet, poor, Asian humanity
sandwiched in between these two great historic streets.

Christmas carols are piped through every speaker.
I see young Chinese saleswomen in those empty shops,
talking to each other in Cantonese,
as they watch the rain drench Grant Avenue.

I know their long hours and low wages.

(Me and my comrades are in the fight for the long haul.)

And I return to the office and finish typing up
an opinion and award
about an older white woman,
a long-term, conscientious, hard-working woman,
who was fired for just cause
because she had attempted to leave the company premises
with 4 pounds of scrap meat.

Whenever You're Cornered, the Only Way Out is to Fight

Karen, comrade and sister poet, sends me this news article
about a woman warrior.
She includes a note that says:
   "We've got her philosophy and her strength, too.
   We'll get them all by the ears and let them have it."

The article is one I've been wanting
to slip into speeches, talks, poems, conversations.
The images we get from reality —
Those fighting-back images in the face of great adversity.

I saw another news article of the Voting Rights marchers.
Their banner, red, black and green — for Black liberation,
carried by Carrie Graves of Richmond, VA — mother of
five teenagers.
Carrie says:
   "My arms are tired, my feet have blisters,
   but I'm fired up!"

So what is *this* article?
The reporter must have loved writing it, the way it came out:

Beijing

   A crippled grandmother caught a leopard by the ears,
dragged it to the ground and then helped kill it with her
bare hands, official reports said Tuesday.

   Qi Deying, who can barely walk because her feet were
bound from birth, was gathering herbs with her niece and
grandchildren on a mountain in North China's Shaanxi
Province when the six-foot leopard attacked her and sank
his teeth into her arm.

But the animal soon realized he had bitten off more than he could chew.

The 77-year-old Qi grabbed the leopard by the ears, wedged its jaw shut with her right shoulder and forced it to the ground, the Shaanxi Daily said.

Their bodies locked in combat, the grandmother and the leopard rolled more than 120 feet down the mountainside, bouncing off rocks before coming to rest in a wheatfield.

Qi called out to her grandchildren, who were hiding behind a boulder, to come to her aid. They tore branches off a tree and helped her beat the animal to death.

Qi, only bruised, told the paper: "Whenever you're cornered, the only way out is to fight."

The Right to Choose

1. The Weakest Link

Why are gay rights and the right to abortion
the weakest link
in bringing all the people
for women's rights together?

Why is fighting abortion and gay rights the door
through which the right-wing   thinks
it will introduce people
to other conservative issues?

> Abortion and gay rights are the most blatant
> expression of women choosing
> themselves first.

> Choosing what to do with their lives
>   and potential —
> Confronting head-on the nuclear family,
>   women's subordination,
>   the Puritan ethic.

Women are supposed to give their lives to others —
      any others: the fetus, men, the boss, the State.
Identified by the man she's married to;
      going with;
      her father and his name;
Judged always by how well she has served others —

> The Private Property Tradition

The bull dyke is disgusting in her independent swagger;
The woman going in for an abortion
      defies in the deepest sense
      the ancient calling to motherhood.

In China, girls were more than valueless —
    a total burden.
Maggots in the rice.
You feed her, clothe her, raise her,
    only to give her away
    as a slave
    to her husband's family.

Is it so different here and now?

The hardest thing to accept is the justice
    of women choosing themselves first.

The poorest man has had it better than
    his female counterpart.

II. Home Sweet Home

She was a Korean office worker in the '50s —
    Had been a domestic
    where her employers counted every single lambchop
    before she went home.

Home was a little oasis
    of peace and acceptance
    with a loving, protective family —

Here she was protected from outside intrusions;
    those rude shattering intrusions:
        racist remarks
        sexist behavior
    being waited on last by the butcher,
    late after a long, long day of work —
    where her boss makes fun of her nose,
        her eyes.

She comes home tired.
    Shuts the door behind her
    a sigh of relief —

Last weekend, she and her husband had gone away,
     "on a little vacation"
     to some mysterious place,
     used their savings
          to go "south."

She comes home tired.
     Puts dinner on the table.
     As she sits down,
     her Catholic daughter says:

"I know where you went.

You went to get an abortion.

You are a murderer
     and will burn in hell."

III. Multiple-Choice Quiz

The following are two statements. Please read them carefully,
and choose the answers that most aptly apply:

A. First Statement:

A human being is in the power of another
with no right to expression of choice
     expression of life
     the potential of that life
no right to choose
     to act freely.

The victim is what the master decides.

Ingratiation/accommodation the norm.

Making demands can mean sudden death.

Possible answers that most fit the description:

1. Slavery.
2. Black South Africa.
The woman, child, elder, disabled, on the Bantustans —
"the superfluous appendages" under white minority rule.
3. The peasants and Indians of Mexico, Central & Latin
America.
4. Undocumented workers; refugees fleeing to this
country.
5. The muted slavery of low-paid women workers in the
field, the plants and factories
of Mission Foods, Watsonville, the Silicon Valley.
6. The rape situation. Or women who are sterilized,
or denied an abortion.
7. Other.
8. All of the above.

B. Second Statement:

We can attain the full right to choose by:

1. Joining the anti-apartheid movement.
2. Working in solidarity with the oppressed peoples
of the *entire* American continent.
3. Fighting the Simpson-Mazzoli anti-immigrant bill.
4. Joining the labor movement: the pickets, demos
for fair working conditions for all.
5. Working in reproductive rights coalitions.
6. Building for a socialist revolution
that is feminist and anti-racist.
7. All of the above.

Presented at the Protect Reproductive Rights Rally,
Richmond, California, September 29, 1985

Jelly Beans

The harmony of a million languages —
Colors never before seen;
People with
Cultures so many so rich always changing
Each with a sense of place
Not ownership.

And also,
We began to see people
Becoming tangible and real,
Becoming their potential.

A thousand-fold of gender expressions —
A wild flourishing of sexualities —

The nuclear family unit had
Dis appeared,
Because everyone had everything
Collectively
Males and females were equal
Children were no longer
Blue and pink incipient workers.

It didn't matter anymore if you
Were mannish or womanish —

Why, you could be
Two spirits, three spirits, four —
Fluid, changing by choice
Or desire,
Merging
Interpenetration of sexualities —
And genders —
For some

Clearly male and female for others —
So many expressions
And speakings out
We no longer laughed at
But admired
The chick who kept her dick —

The tomboy who grew up to be a man,
The tomboy who grew up to be a lesbian,
The tomboy who grew up to be a woman —

The girlboygirl who is still changing
The girl man who is trying to find
The boy he had lost.

We decided that gender expressions
Like racial expressions
Were like jelly beans —
One alone is pretty enough
But one among many
Multi-flavored, multi-colored
Jelly beans
Is
Ecstasy!

Under the
Sword of Damocles

I. Jeopardy

These are wildly proliferating cells, anarchistic,
which engulf and wipe out healthy cells. And in their
rage for expansion and full control, wind up killing
their host and then, of course, themselves.

What is cancer?

II. The Sword

We are breast cancer survivors
Eight of us meeting at the
Women's Cancer Resource Center.

We have survived:
Late diagnosis; misdiagnosis
and bad medical treatment.

One woman says she's tired of
"training doctors."

We have survived surgery:
mastectomies; lumpectomies
chemotherapy and radiation.

Burns and all. . .

Adriamycin which rages thru
the body more angrily than CMF
And CMF:

Hot flashes and baldness
nausea and Irritable Bowel Syndrome

dryness and bleeding in all our orifices
as fast-growing cells are sloughed off.
We experience battle fatigue.

Now, post-treatment,
we are angry and scared as the
sword hangs in delicate balance.

The war in the Persian Gulf
has just begun,

And there is a collective floating anxiety,
death smirks.

On the tv screens:

Oil spills into the Persian Gulf
Fire licks and leaps over the broadening surface
as fowl w/slicked down brown-matted feathers,
blinded,
drag themselves up to the shore.

The amerikan media censors the fact that
300,000 Iraqi are dead;
thus say refugees fleeing into Saudi Arabia.

We are eight angry women
because the u.s. has put our billions
and advanced technology
into stockpiling and using
nuclear weaponry and war mongering
rather than for funding for cancer and
AIDS research.

Our youth, 65% of whom are black brown yellow
are the cannon fodder in the Middle East.

We are tired of being the ground troops
used as guinea pigs/statistics for cancer research.

Tired of ignorant, narrow-minded,
misogynist doctors:
We are keeping and publicizing a list!

III. Mixed Metaphors

I told the group my first night there
that my former lover Karen
died of breast cancer in 1987
at age 40.

And as soon as my life took an
upward turn,
& I found someone to take Karen's place,
I was diagnosed w/breast cancer.

Karen used to say that
whenever she was really happy
she was just waiting for
the rug to be snatched out from under her. . .

Barbara says she's always waiting for
the other shoe to drop.

Did you know that by the time
a tumor is detectable
by touch or by mammogram,
it's been growing for 6 years?

By the time the u.s. hit Iraq
the conservatism
economic depression
racist/sexist repression
had been growing for years.

There are no reliable tests
to detect any recurrences.

Even if chemo is 99.9% successful
that .1% equals 1 million pretty strong contras
— more than enough to start the counter revolution —

No, of course,
we won't give up.
Intent on finding the best treatment
Using Western/Eastern medicine
Whatever works
and passing the information on to others.

In San Francisco,
we were 250,000 protestors strong yesterday.
Marching against an imperialist war —
people taking power.

So why should we be still
sitting under the sword of Damocles?

Mumia Imagines Freedom

Mumia imagines Freedom.
He sits there in his cell
on Death Row,
Imagining Freedom.

He imagines Freedom
for all who are in prison and silenced by their race, sex,
    sexuality and class
and their political beliefs —

This brave Black brother
has a plan —
To free not only himself
But us all!

Capitalism keeps us all in chains —

Capitalism and its right-hand man, imperialism,
causes:
wars, unionbusting, pollution, the prison industrial complex,
sexism, homophobia, racism, anti-immigrant scapegoating,
national chauvinism —

Mumia's freedom plan is revolution!

He says "Revolution is not a word but an application; it is not
war but peace; it does not weaken, but strengthens. Revolution
does not cause separation but generates togetherness."

This very great movement — to free an innocent man
who's been on death row for twenty years
because he has been honest and outspoken about his plans for
our freedom —

This movement that we are building here and all over the world,
where at least 70 countries have come out in support of him —

is the biggest movement and *longest* to come along since the anti-Vietnam war.

But this movement is going to be even greater than the anti-Vietnam war movement because it is not single-issue but multi-issue;
this movement is all inclusive.
And it is anti-capitalist and radical —
because of Mumia Abu-Jamal.

All you young people out there.
If you've talked about how you missed the sixties,
its activism and the anti-war movement,
well here you are now in a movement just as big but broader.
You are on the crest of a wave that is turning into a revolution.

Mumia is my Black Brother. He has defended women.
He talks about Ella Baker's leadership in the civil rights movement and building SNCC.
He credits her leadership as she exposed the sexual exploitation of poor women,
working as domestics.
Another extension of slavery!
He also defended a radical lesbian journalist who was fired.

Freedom ain't gonna come from the Democrats or the
     Republicans,
Tweedledum and Tweedledummer.

And it's not going to be Ralph Nader.
He's only going skin-deep,
focusing on a few corporations —
when the problem is the whole damn system!

We must begin now to create the united fronts,
with us in the leadership,
democracy will be needed
to defend our livelihoods, our rights and our natural resources.

Remember what Mumia said: "Criticize! Viable, radical, and revolutionary parties should also be organized and energized to provide real, meaningful alternatives."

Mumia imagines Freedom
And plans Revolt!

FREE MUMIA!
FREE MUMIA!
FREE OURSELVES!

Presented at the rally to Free Mumia Abu-Jamal and All Political Prisoners at Staples Center, Los Angeles, CA, August 13, 2000.

Transgenderism:
The Essential Challenge

You might say that our
society has acknowledged. . .finally
three categories of human sexuality:
straight, gay, and bi

But what about transgenderism —
which fills out the rest of the sexual spectrum
— perhaps unrelated to sexual preference —
which is potent in its challenge to
Patriarchal Capitalism?

How will the status quo continue
to reinforce women's free labor in the home
which justifies their being underpaid at the workplace?
72¢ on the dollar a man makes for white women,
and even less for women of color and disabled women?

How will women's inferiority be reinforced —
The cult of motherhood and servitude —
If you can't tell the difference?

Polymorphously Perverse

Aggressive. Oh, you'll see.
You won't know from where or to what —
Where will you find me wiggling my ear?
Shall I put my foot in the palm of your hand?
Bolder. . . bolder. . .
Where will I put my shoulder?

> (You fascinate me so.
> Apricot oil on our bellies,
> rubbing back and forth together.)

Will you be driving and suddenly find
a finger in your ear or
a tongue on a button?

> (I love rubbing my front
> against your sweet bottom,
> Love your top in my front,
> my hand caressing a breast
> that will not be confined by a bra.
> Sometimes I come when you do,
> Just from loving you.)

CAUTION:
Areas to watch out for:

Don't park in isolated areas of airport parking lots.
(She's been starving for you.)

Don't go into the bathroom.
(She will follow and grab and hug and kiss. . .)

Avoid crowds.
(For she will use this opportunity to sidle up,
encircle, a touch under a jacket.

Watch out for elbows and arms
that must brush the fullness of breasts.)

And she'll wear sunglasses even if it's pouring
so she can stare at places with impunity.

    A hip urging a thigh
    Breathe your whispering softness in
    Smell the lightning
    Taste the pulses, 1,2,3,4.
    Then, thunder.

This pleasure/curiosity —
All the innocence,
openness
sensuousness
of new born babes.

Under a Full Moon

In the deepest night and a full moon,
at once riding the flying mare and being her,
my own pumping broad wings, ascending higher —

My legs around that great horse's neck
not riding
but my body singing down under,
in front of the beautiful dark head —
feeling her moist tongue in my center —

I am risking my life for these moments,
My head possibly dashed against the rocks.

Now riding with our rhythms matching,
the exertion of her back's muscles and
the mounting pulsations between my thighs —

Higher and soaring through mist and above mountains
Shaped like jagged spires —
The cold thin air ripping through my lungs —

We finish.
And you lay your head on my thigh,
your wings enfolding my legs, and we rest.

You are Special

You are the sea
the fresh meadow grass
lush planet Venus —

Soft Strong
pliant like good silver
as hard as revolution makes.
I want to polish you
with my tongue
until you're shining
          ecstatic
your hands grabbing my hair
pulling me into you.

We are not one
but one as two
Double the pleasure
Double the fight.

Responsibilities of Freedom

Those of us who have chosen the path less traveled
Abandoning values of capitalism and patriarchy

Are freedom fighters
And at the same time so free

That without our comrades' criticism
We may repeat the old
Harmful inhumane ways we treat others

Can we see leadership in the most disenfranchised?
Can we build new personal and collective lives
Unaffected by internal competition, jealousy, and power?

Are our lives less painful, less filled with struggle?
Indeed not
For freedom demands responsibility and
Constant consciousness

In political work, we welcome free and open debate internally —
Externally, we're a solid clenched fist in the air.

But what about the personal?
That undefined herstory that needs re-creation
Creativity, objectivity, consciousness
Not bound to memory, bad experiences, addictions
Of our past

In our freedom

No revolutionary can abandon
The personal life, the joys of supportive friends,
families, and lovers
We do have those.

But sometimes our loved ones do not support what we do
    and believe
We struggle for their respect and make compromises

In the absence of clear road signs
In our freedom,
We seek approval and acceptance —
At the same time we have had to create
Our own gauges of better human relations
Comradeship. Morality.

Often I feel such self-doubt
Paranoia almost

On my off days, hard-won victories turn upside down

Having no job security
Hounded from job to job
Threatens my self-confidence
Chronic illness
Threatens my self-confidence

As I near my 60th birthday
I intend to have my own recommitment ceremony
To this freedom.

The hardest to change
Is to attach no blame
Or judgment to what I
Consider to be an unfair criticism —

If someone disses me
I want to go on the offensive
I want to focus on the hurt done to me
Rather than ask what motivated that
Comment and ask kind questions and listen.

Then *that* gets muddled with suspicion
Doubts about how other comrades perceive me or regard me.

In our own little group of warriors
Always going against the grain
How do we know what's right
If not by our comrades' loving criticism
Which can hurt —
Especially when we are weak in evaluating
Our own worth

There is pain in realizing
That in this area of socialist human relations
I have been impatient,
Not understanding —
Judgmental and angry

In this freedom we have so much power
We'd be given even more leadership if we wanted it.

Only by being a radical in this oppressive for-profit society
Can we come close to realizing our human potential
But we must constantly struggle for it —

Freedom means responsibility
For making better choices
Based on new consciousness,
Like the common good and self-defense —
Our comrades
Our socialist feminist theory and program.

We determine not to mimic
The oppressive negative behavior of our past
When that's all we knew —

Taking the path less trodden
Clearing the way responsibly
For others to trust and be hopeful
Optimistic about our human future — flourishing!

Eulogy

When Ma died
I was shocked that at 51 years
I could feel so much grief
and guilt —
Would I ever get over her passing?

Since my world was fashioned
by my mother
where not a day would go by
without my thinking about her
about what she would say —

Would I have to recreate the whole world
this time in my own image?

We have faced the same oppressions
but our resistance has been
polar opposites:

hers inward, turning inward
becoming an isolate;
mine, because of hers,
outward, turning outward
becoming a revolutionary feminist.

She provided the knowledge
and a perspective of the world

and if my direction became
opposite from hers —
if I have chosen a way
which when I die
I won't have regrets,

it was because of her
always because of her.

Yellow Woman Speaks

Shadow become real; follower become leader;
    mouse turned sorcerer —

In a red sky, a darker beast lies waiting,
    her teeth, once hidden, now unsheathed swords.

Yellow woman, a revolutionary, speaks:

"They have mutilated our genitals, but I will restore them;
I will render our shames and praise them,
Our beauties, our mothers:
Those young Chinese whores on display in barracoons;
the domestics in soiled aprons;
the miners, loggers, railroad workers
    holed up in Truckee in winters.
            I will create armies of their descendants.

And I will expose the lies and ridicule
the impotence of those who have called us
    chink
    yellow-livered
    slanted cunts
    exotic
in order to abuse and exploit us.
            And I will destroy them."

Abrasive teacher, incisive comedienne,
Painted Lady, dark domestic —
Sweep minds' attics; burnish our senses;
keep house, make love, wreak vengeance.

On the Front Line of Freedom

And who will be with me on the Front Line of Freedom?

Will it be the white lesbians and gays who oppress
    people of color,
    the poor and disadvantaged?

Will it be the people of color,
    my people,
    my Asian brothers and sisters who hate and despise gays?
    who look with disgust upon me,
    who see my lover as a ghost? a devil?

Will it be working men who are sexist? Who treat me with
    disrespect,
    call me names because I am a woman?
    An Asian woman?
    A Chinky China Doll? A Slant Cunt?
    Comparing me to a pug dog? with buck teeth?
    Dehumanizing me?

Will we be on the Front Line Together?
I don't think so.

And yet, I am fighting for the rights of just these people
    who oppress me.
Because I am a lesbian mother, an Asian, and a worker.

I stand with those who are the most enslaved —
    who have no say in the determination of
    their bodies' choices;
    their minds' wills.

Face to Face:
The Right Wing on the Front Line of Slavery calls their
    continued bondage:

Population Control
Family Protection Act
the Moral Majority —
Just listen to the White House Fathers on the Human Life
Amendment.

On the Front Line of Freedom. . .
I march and stand with all the women of color who have
    been sterilized:
    80% of the tribe in Oklahoma
    so that the U.S. will inherit (in one generation)
    the earth, rich with Uranium,
    gold for nuclear weaponry;
    42% of all Native American women,
    35% of all Puerto Rican women,
    25% of all Chicanas — have been sterilized —

(And of course you know that in 1945, a motion was up
before Congress to have all Japanese American women,
who were interned, sterilized; it lost by only one vote.)

    Those poor young women of color who go in to
    deliver a baby and come out sterilized.

    Those who go in for an abortion and can't have one.

I stand with the Black mothers and fathers of the children
    of Atlanta;
    The Black parents in Oakland whose babies are dying;

I march with the poor lesbians and gays who have
    no legal aid;
    who don't know what it's like to eat Veal Piccata and
    Chocolate Mousse Torte at Fife's on the Russian River;

    The ones who hurt the most —
    Who can't keep cool on summer days,
    picking shells by the seashore,

Who can't keep warm winter's nights, with chestnuts
roasting by an open fire —

Who don't know what it means to have a regular
checkup.

The old who are poor and sick and lonely, shunted from one
hospital to another.
Maybe a hip broken, and sometimes the spirit.

MediCal gals and guys.

I stand with the physically disabled.

And the clerical workers who type in asbestos offices (as if
they had a choice),
the factory workers who get brown lung disease
the electronic production workers who are slowly dying
in the Silicon Valley, because of constant exposure to
noxious chemicals/carcinogens.

I stand with political prisoners, and those falsely accused and
confined to penitentiaries
because of the laws which protect the rich.

Because of the history of my people in this country,
I stand with those who cannot immigrate because of race,
sexuality, lack of profession, political persuasion.

We are called the Undesirables.

Finally, I stand with those who may not be oppressed because
of their race, sex, sexuality, physicality, class, or age,
but who know why discrimination exists and will attack
the source: Capitalism.

I love the word "socialism"
because of the root, "social"
a focus on social relationships, community

and the freedom to associate, recreate,
rather than on capital and class, profit and not people.

I love the word "feminism"
    because when I say, think, and act it,
    I mean multi-issue
    Revolutionary Feminism, which attacks
    white
    patriarchal
    mr. amerika
    judeo-christian
    heterosexual
    models of hierarchy and exploitation
    that hold all women, men of color, poor, and gay men
    back and inferior,
    and with unfulfilled potential.

I march, stand, and fight with socialist feminists because
    in its purest
    most fulfilled definition
    in theory and action,
    it is Revolutionary Feminism which is a
    fight for everyone who is oppressed
    in one way or another
    and which has as its goal
    the certainty that

Those on the Front Line of Freedom will inherit the Earth.

Presented at the Lesbian, Gay, Bisexual Pride Parade and Rally,
San Francisco, CA, June 1981.

Merle Woo is a socialist feminist educator and writer, who is currently teaching in Women's Studies at San Jose State University.

For 20 years, Merle has been a leader in Radical Women and the Freedom Socialist Party. During the '80s, as an outspoken Marxist lesbian feminist, she won an unfair labor practice (represented by the American Federation of Teachers), an out-of-court settlement, and a union arbitration by AFT against the University of California for violation of her free speech rights and discrimination based on race, sex, sexuality and political ideology.

In the 1990s, Merle fought with lecturers and students to maintain student democracy, and a lesbian and community focus in Women Studies at San Francisco State University.

Merle received the humanitarian award from the Northern California Lesbian and Gay Historical Society in 1994. Today she is a member of the California Faculty Association and the Mobilization to Free Mumia Abu-Jamal.

INTRODUCING
RADICAL WOMEN

This trailblazing socialist feminist organization is the revolutionary wing of the women's movement and a strong feminist voice within the Left. Immersed in the daily fight against racism, sexism, homophobia, and labor exploitation, Radical Women views women's leadership as decisive to global change.

If you share these interests, become a member! From mass action to mass mailings, from publicity to public speaking, from coalition-building to cooking, everyone has something to learn, teach, and contribute in Radical Women!

Contact the Radical Women National Office
for information about the branch nearest you:
New Freeway Hall, 5018 Rainier Ave. S.
Seattle, WA 98118
Phone: (206)722-6057• Fax: (206)723-7691
RadicalWomenUS@gmail.com • www.radicalwomen.org

THE RADICAL WOMEN MANIFESTO:
SOCIALIST FEMINIST THEORY, PROGRAM AND ORGANIZATIONAL STRUCTURE

"Radical Women brings vision, militancy, and an ethic of collaboration to the feminist movement, and we have been influential far beyond our size. RW has moved public discourse as a whole to the left, toward attention to the needs and demands of the most excluded and harassed members of society. In so doing, the organization has magnified the strength and effectiveness of the feminist, labor, people of color and lesbian/gay struggles.

"I fell in love with Radical Women for its passion, boldness, imagination, intelligence and principle. All these qualities are as fresh today as they were the day I joined. ...Connect with us in the great adventure of creating a socialist feminist future!"

—*Introduction by Megan Cornish*

"Radical Women is dedicated to exposing, resisting and eliminating the inequities of women's existence. To accomplish this task of insuring survival for an entire sex, we must simultaneously address ourselves to the social and material source of sexism: the capitalist form of production and distribution of products, characterized by intrinsic class, race, sex, ethnic and caste oppression. When we work for the revolutionary transformation of capitalism into a socialist society, we work for a world in which *all* people may enjoy the right of full humanity and freedom from poverty, war, racism, sexism, anti-Semitism, and repression.

"We believe that the liberation of women is indissolubly linked to the battle against all the burning injustices that define capitalism. ...[We] cannot isolate our struggle by creating a single-issue movement that ignores the multifaceted reality of women's oppression. All oppressed groups are fighting the same enemy. We must build a movement that can bring our separate struggles together. Unified we become strong."

—*The Radical Women Manifesto*

$8.00 U.S./**$10.00** Canada & Australia
$1.50 shipping per copy

Order from **Radical Women Publications**
5018 Rainier Avenue South • Seattle, WA 98118, USA
(206)722-6057 • Fax (206)723-7691 • www.radicalwomen.org